MW01001971

FACE YOUR FEARS

LEARNING TO TRUST GOD IN SCARY TIMES

ED TAYLOR

Face Your Fears By: Ed Taylor

Abounding Grace Media
18900 E. HAMPDEN AVE. AURORA, CO 80013
(303) 628-7200

Here you are reading a book on fear. There were many choices when looking for a new book to read, but fear is still the topic. You're tired of your fears and anxieties controlling you. You're tired of cowering away from God's purposes for your life. You're tired of going backward in your relationship with Jesus and sense it's time to "face your fears." It's a blessing that you're in a place where you're ready to be encouraged. You've made a wise choice.

Fear and anxiety have exponentially increased among us over the past year. On top of all the usual and challenging issues, we face daily, a pandemic with economic uncertainties and confusing mixed messages was thrust upon us and messed us up. If that weren't all, you could add to the mix painful divisions, isolation, confrontations, an unexpected medical diagnosis, major life changes, and a new atmosphere of senseless choices, which have made things much worse.

How could we not experience some sort of fear in times like these? Fear, it's real, isn't it? The New Oxford Dictionary defines fear as "an unpleasant emotion caused by the belief that someone or something is dangerous, likely to cause pain or a threat;" and "(fear for) a feeling of anxiety concerning the outcome of something or the safety and well-being of someone;" and "the likelihood of something unwelcome happening." Those are heavy words! Reading them might have stirred up some fresh fear in your heart right now! We can be fragile at times.

ORIGINS OF FEAR

Fear. Anxiety. Depression. Unwelcome. Threats. Who wants to live with these every day? *I know you don't.* When you hear others speak of their courage and confidence, that's what you want too. (If it were only that easy.) I'm glad that you're deciding to face your fears head-on. Your decision is met with God's power! He is faithful to meet you in your deepest and weakest times. Your choice to face your fears will be met with God's faithful presence. His perfect love casts out all fear. Isn't that encouraging? It is!

I'm sure you have had a well-meaning friend come to you in the midst of your fears and quote to you this beautiful verse from the Bible:

"For God has not given us a spirit of fear, but of power and of love and of a sound mind."(2 Timothy 1:7)

It is a glorious truth to hang on to, friend. Be careful not to be defensive and start to defend the very fears that have overwhelmed you. God has given us a wonderful reminder of how important it is to know where fear comes from. You should memorize this verse right away.

Overwhelming fear originates when we no longer live with the consciousness of God. I say overwhelming because not all fear is bad. God created the emotion of fear in order to warn us of impending dangers and move us to safer places. Normal fear unchecked quickly becomes irrational. When we allow fear to cloud our minds, it causes great anxiety, and its evidence that we have lost the sense of God's presence in our lives. To describe this, we sometimes will say that you 'have your eyes off the Lord'. When you are living independently of seeing, knowing, and believing that God is with you, this 'spirit' of fear rises, and before you know it, it overtakes your mind.

Irrational and faithless fears do not come from our abiding relationship with Jesus. What Jesus has for you and me today is power, love, and a sound mind. He is faithful to us.

STUCK

We all deal with fear from time to time. God has given us this critical emotion for good reasons. But there are those times when our regular and normal fears become illogical and unreasonable. They lead us to make bad decisions that only make things worse. Feeling trapped and stuck is no fun at all. Perhaps that's you. You feel stuck. You feel like there is no way out. You may feel stuck in your marriage or your singleness, or your job.

The good news is that you're not stuck. God is with you and can make a way where there is no way. Many situations in life leave us thinking that there is no way out. We falsely conclude that this is the end. We don't know what's going to happen. We don't see any future up ahead. Daily we live with a variety of dangers, hazards, and difficulties that stir up debilitating fears and anxieties. It's easy to be gripped by and paralyzed by unjustifiable fears that lead to deep discouragement and a sense of being overwhelmed by it all.

That's part of the problem. You're stuck in your own head, listening to your own reasoning, surrounded by your own thoughts, and that's not making things any better. Maybe you're even beginning to isolate yourself and pull away from people that love you and want to help you. You just don't want to hear any more Bible verses! *You don't want to listen to any more well-meaning advice!* No more trite prayers, you say. That leaves you in a greater place of danger since now all you're hearing is yourself. You are concluding that God isn't there and people don't care, which has depleted your hope and sapped your faith leaving you living on razor-thin margins. You falsely think that God doesn't care and He's unavailable to meet your needs. It's a recipe for disaster and destruction. Yes, God loves you and cares for you. You need to hear that and cling to Him. He is the Good Shepherd who is with you always.

"Yea, though I walk through the valley of the shadow of death, I will fear no evil; For You are with me; Your rod and Your staff, they comfort me."
(Psalm 23:4)

Fear coupled with anxiety is a dangerous mixture of volatile emotions. These two emotions can often cause an otherwise rational, logical person to do a lot of senseless and illogical things.   Sometimes you choose not to listen to the Word of God. Other times you chose to run away from problems and avoid difficult situations. Making things worse is a culture filled with all sorts of narratives surrounding current events and the future.   The world's view of things is typically negative, by the way. That doesn't help. It seems like everyone wants a piece of your ear. They want you to believe them and follow them as they capitalize on your fears. Listening to them actually makes things worse. You get more confused, not less.

God wants us to walk by faith, trusting in Him day by day. He is capable of taking care of our every need. He has gone before us and knows what we will face, preparing us for it. It's time to choose to trust God, friend. Choose to trust Him right now and create a new habit of trusting Him over and over again. Solomon, filled with the wisdom of God, wrote:

"The fear of man brings a snare, But whoever trusts in the LORD shall be safe."(Proverbs 29:25)

The word fear here is the Hebrew word, "*haradah*," which means 'trembling, quaking, and fear.' It's used of the terror of God that overcame the enemy (1 Samuel 14:15) and the fear that startled Daniel's friends in a vision (Daniel 10:7). But it also refers to an unjustifiable fear developed when we fear man. The fear of man comes in a variety of ways. It can be a fear of their position, what they can do to us, or even what they say. It doesn't matter how fear is generated, and the Bible says it brings a trap and a snare into our lives. When you and I are snared, our forward progress is impaired. The snare is where we can get caught up in the currents of our culture and are taken away from our abiding relationship in Jesus.   Your fear of man is holding you back from God's best in your life. You are again entangled and held back.

WHERE DO WE TURN

It's not hard to get caught up in the emotion of it all. Things are not as they should be because of sin and the sinful decisions of others. That freaks us out, and we are held back, stuck. Our greatest enemy many times is actually ourselves. The battle for clarity is real. The battle for clarity is in our minds. Who will we choose to trust? Who will we turn to when times are hard? It's only in God's Word do we find the stability of hope that anchors our life in Christ.

"This is my comfort in my affliction, For Your word has given me life."(Psalm 119:50)

It's worth mentioning again that the emotion of fear is real. **Your emotion of fear is real.** I recognize and acknowledge your real fears. We want to be careful not to minimize the reality of what you're feeling. But even with your real fears, you want to learn to take that fear to the Lord. *You want to learn to saturate your entire being with the Word of God. You want to learn to encourage yourself in the Lord. You want to develop a regular prayer and devotional life so that you are continually running to the Lord with your emotions.* Why? Because fear will absolutely rob you of your faith and trust in God. Fear is not to be nurtured or coddled. *We must choose to not feed our fears.* **We must choose to feed our faith!** Your irrational fears are to be dealt a death blow by believing in God and trusting Him, moment by moment, day by day. Years ago, Harry Fosdick shared great insight on the contrast between faith and fear. He wrote, *"Fear imprisons, faith liberates; fear paralyzes, faith empowers; fear disheartens, faith encourages; fear sickens, faith heals; fear makes useless, faith makes serviceable-and, most of all, fear puts hopelessness at the heart of life, while faith rejoices in its God."* Isn't that true?! I have learned over the years that knowing and experiencing and abiding in the love of God indeed does cast out all fear.

"There is no fear in love; but perfect love casts out fear, because fear involves torment. But he who fears has not been made perfect in love. We love Him because He first loved us."(1 John 4:18–19)

DELIVERED

Throughout the Bible, there are many examples of God's deliverance of people gripped by unfounded fears. As we look back to a time in the life of the nation of Israel, I hope you are strengthened in hope. That's God's desire for you; to have your fears replaced with faith, to have your anxiety replaced with confidence, to have your hopelessness replaced with hope.

"Now the LORD spoke to Moses, saying: *"Speak to the children of Israel, that they turn and camp before Pi Hahiroth, between Migdol and the sea, opposite Baal Zephon; you shall camp before it by the sea. For Pharaoh will say of the children of Israel, 'They are bewildered by the land; the wilderness has closed them in.' Then I will harden Pharaoh's heart, so that he will pursue them; and I will gain honor over Pharaoh and over all his army, that the Egyptians may know that I am the LORD."* And they did so.

Now it was told the king of Egypt that the people had fled, and the heart of Pharaoh and his servants was turned against the people; and they said, "Why have we done this, that we have let Israel go from serving us?"

So he made ready his chariot and took his people with him. Also, he took six hundred choice chariots, and all the chariots of Egypt with captains over every one of them. *And the LORD hardened the heart of Pharaoh king of Egypt, and he pursued the children of Israel, and the children of Israel went out with boldness.* So the Egyptians pursued them, all the horses and chariots of Pharaoh, his horsemen and his army, and overtook them camping by the sea beside Pi Hahiroth, before Baal Zephon."(Exodus 14:1–9)

In the book of Exodus chapter 14, we meet a group of people, perhaps a few million that have just been miraculously delivered from horrific bondage as slaves in Egypt. When we think millions, we must pause for a moment and remember that each one has a name, a family, and a story to tell. These are boys and girls, moms and dads, grandmas and grandpas. They are not nameless unimportant people gripped with fear but precious people for whom God acted on their behalf!

It's good to be reminded that you too, are *not* a nameless unimportant person. You are loved and known by God *personally*. Soak that in for a moment. *He knows your fears and loves you supremely. He's ready to deliver you too.*

Just before their deliverance, the nation of Israel had been crying out for help, crying out to God for His delivering power. God answers "YES" and sends a man by the name of Moses to face Pharoah head-on. He does. He is God's deliverer! As Moses stands before the ruler of the known world in the authority of God, he is used as a mouthpiece to Pharaoh demanding the nation's release. It's a fascinating and true story. *(You should go back and reread Exodus. You will be encouraged.)* Eventually, Pharoah gives in and expels the nation of Israel out of Egypt. They pick up and leave, by the millions—what a deliverance.

If you were to take out a Bible map and trace the route God led this nation out of Egypt and toward the land to which He promised them, you might notice that there were other options available than the one God chose. The one God chose for them led them into a seeming trap. There were many more convenient and safer ways to leave Egypt, but they were led to one that left them stuck.

There is that word again, **"stuck."** You see, you're not the only one that feels stuck. It's a familiar feeling and almost always untrue.

Here is this fledgling nation, moments ago under the harsh reality of slavery, deep pain, and suffering, now free, getting out of Egypt as fast as they can. They have wholeheartedly committed themselves to the care of God under the leadership of Moses. God leads, and they follow. They stop. Now they are stuck. They are stuck but by the will of God. Before them is the Red Sea. Large mountains are on either side of them. And the fast-approaching Egyptian army is pressing in hard from behind them. It was their fear that blinded them from the truths that not only was God still with them but that this was His will for their lives. It was what we call a Divine setup.

"And when Pharaoh drew near, the children of Israel lifted their eyes, and behold, the Egyptians marched after them. So they were very afraid, and the children of Israel cried out to the LORD. Then they said to Moses, *"Because there were no graves in Egypt, have you taken us away to die in the wilderness? Why have you so dealt with us, to bring us up out of Egypt? Is this not the word that we told you in Egypt, saying, 'Let us alone that we may serve the Egyptians'? For it would have been better for us to serve the Egyptians than that we should die in the wilderness."*
(Exodus 14:10–12)

PANIC AND DECISIONS

Pharoah, I believe, began to have second thoughts about letting his free workforce leave the country. Being the ruthless leader he was, he chases after them with the best of the best of his military. As the nation of Israel sees their situation getting worse, the Bible says they were terrified. This is a real, rational fear. It's the same feeling you and I would have had if we were in that situation. Of course, they are afraid. But their response isn't as clean as it seems. We tend to read the Bible with "Christian" eyes thinking the best in all situations. It says they 'cried out to the Lord'. We immediately think, yes, that's the right choice. Good job, people. But I don't think that's what happened here. I believe they cried out to God not in hope but in anger and irrational fear. They are desperate and faithless. Panicked reactions so quickly corrupted their faith. What started as a real fear quickly developed into irrational fear. We see the same thing in our lives. Our fundamental problem is our refusal to believe God in a crisis. When things are ok, then we are ok. But when a crisis arises, we panic. ***When we panic, we make many bad decisions.***

Look at how they treated poor Moses. Remember, this is all happening within a few days. They've gone from excitement and joy to anger, frustration, and regret, all because they choose to let their fear run wild. They tell Moses, "Weren't there any graves in Egypt? Why have you taken us into Egypt?" What? This is what they cried out to God for day after day for years! They are literally living on answered prayer. They are out. They are delivered. But once they face an impossible scary situation, their faith in God and his leader is lost, and now they are upset and want to undo all that God has done! Outrageous, you think? It's more common than you realize.

It was *not* better for them to remain in Egypt. It was *not* better for them to return to Egypt and live there until they died and filled up those empty graves. It was *not* right for them to pressure Moses. It was *not* right for them to doubt God. But this is the human condition. What's not right for them is not right for you and me either. You need to know that. *The bad decisions you are making because of your unsound fears are not right.* **God is ready to deliver you.**

The children of Israel faced a very challenging situation but failed to see the spiritual side of things. Where they are right now is the exact place where God is going to do something incredible. It was not better for them to give up on the faithfulness of God. This is the exact time God has ordained for them to walk in victory and move on to better things. *It's not time to retreat. It's not time to be angry with those God has put into your life to help you and lead you. In times of great fear, you must choose to trust in the Lord!*

There are two things to watch out for in your life as you choose to serve God by serving His people. First, understand that some people may become angry, fearful, and foolish when times get difficult. Secondly, understand there is a very good chance that you will be treated like Moses was treated here. As the volume of murmuring and complaining increases, you will be blamed for all the difficulties in a person's life.

Are you like the children of Israel, angry, frustrated, and lashing out at those closest to you? Are you murmuring and complaining instead of trusting and waiting?

REPENTANCE IS NEEDED

The proper response to our irrational fears is repentance, a true change of mind, a real change of heart. **Irrational fears that lead to not trusting God are sinful.** There is only one thing to do when fears have caused you to sin. Repent. You need to choose to change your mind, heart, and actions by turning away from your sin and asking for God's forgiveness.

"Now I rejoice, not that you were made sorry, but that your sorrow led to repentance. For you were made sorry in a godly manner, that you might suffer loss from us in nothing. For godly sorrow produces repentance leading to salvation, not to be regretted; but the sorrow of the world produces death."(2 Corinthians 7:9–10)

Your repentance will break the cycle of the bad decisions that follow faithlessness. It's not enough to recognize it. We must go all the way and forsake it. Through humble repentance, you can live without being controlled by unfounded fears in your life. God has led you to this place so that He might show His power and majesty in your life.

Our habitual focus on the difficulties surrounding our lives makes us forget the sovereignty of God. Sovereignty is a Bible word that describes God's absolute power and control over the affairs of man. Many Christians are looking at the world today with all its uncertainty and just throwing up their hands in despair as if God doesn't exist. Those on the outside look at the Church today and ask, "doesn't anybody believe in God anymore?" I do! I'm encouraging you to believe in God's power too. God is going to use the difficult things in your life right now to purify you, change you, and move you in preparation for what's up ahead. Nothing is wasted by God. I wrote a whole chapter in my book **"God's Help for the Troubled Heart"** to remind us that nothing is wasted by God. He works all things together for His glory and your good.

No matter how hard it is right now, you don't need to be mad at God or mad with the spiritual leaders in your life. Choose not to look to the left, or look to the right, or look down. Instead, choose to look up, for your redemption draws near!

"Now when these things begin to happen, look up and lift up your heads, because your redemption draws near."(Luke 21:28)

DEEPER FAITH

Another thing God is doing through the difficult times is taking you to a new level of faith. He doesn't want you to go backward but rather to press on forward. It's possible that things in your life will not get better but may get worse. Then what? Then, we must choose to endure the difficulties by faith. God wants to stir us up. He wants to bring you from glory to glory and strength to strength. He's brought to this place to take you beyond it.

"For you have need of endurance, so that after you have done the will of God, you may receive the promise:"(Hebrews 10:36)

What is the root of your irrational fears? Are you afraid of losing something? *Is it fair to say you are fearful of losing your comfort and ease?* Are you afraid of losing privileges and securities? *Every moment we live trying to protect temporary things is a moment that erodes our daily trust in the Lord.* **Commit to trust in the Lord.** Repeat it daily in your prayers.

"In this manner, therefore, pray: Our Father in heaven, Hallowed be Your name. Your kingdom come. Your will be done On earth as it is in heaven. Give us this day our daily bread. And forgive us our debts, As we forgive our debtors. And do not lead us into temptation, But deliver us from the evil one. For Yours is the kingdom and the power and the glory forever. Amen."(Matthew 6:9–13)

I appreciate the example of Moses in this situation as he absorbed the murmuring and complaining, which I believe was loud and scary, with great poise and calmness.

"And Moses said to the people, *"Do not be afraid. Stand still, and see the salvation of the LORD, which He will accomplish for you today.* For the Egyptians whom you see today, you shall see again no more forever. The LORD will fight for you, and you shall hold your peace."(Exodus 14:13–14)

Moses' response to the people was one of strong faith and authority. Let me paraphrase Moses' answer for you in words that are a little more understandable. Basically, Moses told the people, ***"Stand still. Be Quiet. See God Work."*** These are three helpful instructions for you and me too.

First, stand still. Stop trying to squirm out of the situation. Stop looking backward. Calm down. Breathe. Slow your roll. You get the point.

"Be still, and know that I am God; I will be exalted among the nations, I will be exalted in the earth! The LORD of hosts is with us; The God of Jacob is our refuge. Selah"(Psalm 46:10–11)

Secondly, be quiet. You must quiet down. Stop murmuring and complaining. Also, stop the negative talk. Say nothing. You'll never hear the voice of the Lord if you don't first quiet down.

"For thus says the Lord GOD, the Holy One of Israel: "In returning and rest you shall be saved; In quietness and confidence shall be your strength." But you would not,"(Isaiah 30:15)

Thirdly, look for God to work. He's ready to fight for you. He's with you still. Look for Him in the situation and trust Him.

"The Jews answered Him, saying, "For a good work we do not stone You, but for blasphemy, and because You, being a Man, make Yourself God."(John 10:33)

Why are these three things so important in a season of irrational fear? You know what happens. We try to control things. For some, that translates into super frantic negative controlling behaviors. For others, it will even lead to sinful manipulation of others to get a sense and feeling of security. When you think you have control in an uncontrollable situation, it gives you a false sense of comfort. The problem is not in feeling comfort but rather the problem is that you trust in yourself instead of trusting in the Lord. You are relying upon your own limited resources and not upon the infinite resources of God.

The Bible teaches us that God is the God of **"ALL"** comfort. True comfort comes from Him, not our little schemes and devices. As you are trying to fix this, and settle that and control her, you're not at all in place of God's comfort. Stand still. Be Quiet. Look to God.

"Blessed be the God and Father of our Lord Jesus Christ, the Father of mercies and God of all comfort, who comforts us in all our tribulation, that we may be able to comfort those who are in any trouble, with the comfort with which we ourselves are comforted by God."(2 Corinthians 1:3–4)

Moses encourages me here because he doesn't even know what is going to happen yet. He is in the same place as everyone else. He simply chose to respond a different way. I love that! It reminds me that no matter what is going on around me and no matter how loud the crowds are, I can choose to respond by faith in Jesus and trust Him with the situation!

FAITH IS ESSENTIAL

Moses is speaking words of faith to a faithless people. If you are a man or woman of faith, we need you! The encouragement of the Lord through you is so needed in the Body of Christ today. We need you to speak words of faith to us in our faithless condition. Unfortunately, the false teaching of the "faith movement" has made many so scared to live and speak by faith. We reject the false teachings of the "prosperity gospel" teachers for sure. But we need you to live out your faith, so it encourages us. Speak words of faith to us so we can get back on track with Jesus

Faith is essential. *True faith comes from God.* God strengthens you in your faith. He reveals Himself as reliable, and we respond by trusting Him. He encourages you in your faith, and when faith comes from your life, you encourage us! We need you!!! Did I say that already? *In times of great fear and illogical anxiety, we need to walk by faith because there are always times when we are faithless.*

"If we are faithless, He remains faithful; He cannot deny Himself."(2 Timothy 2:13)

Moses tells the people that "The Lord will fight for you." He is on your side. In your fear today, right now, you need to get your eyes back on the Lord. I'm sure reading this book is your step toward doing just that. Great!

God has led you to this situation, allowed it in your life so that you will experience a deeper relationship with Him. He is your great Deliverer. Like Moses and the nation of Israel here, you can choose to look to the obstacles in your life, or you can look to the Lord.

Please don't get me wrong; the obstacles are real and scary. Of course, they are, or they would have never stumbled you along the way. What you choose to focus on will determine the direction of your life.

You will never get to enjoy what God is doing and going to do in your life when you're worried about the Egyptians (problems, difficulties, and issues). When the enemy of God shapes the narrative of your life, it leads to misery and anguish. He's a liar. God is truth.

There is a genuine chance you will experience even more difficult things than what you are going through right now. The Bible teaches us that as the return of Jesus gets closer and closer, that things are earth will get harder and harder. Situations will be more challenging.

Here's what happens. Instead of responding with faith, we demand an answer to why bad things are happening in our lives. You start saying things like, "I just don't know why God is doing this." With that little question, you get stuck once again, thinking that if you can get a good answer to that question, you can move on, move forward.

Are you asking that question today? My simple answer is, "I don't know exactly what God is doing in your life. But I do know this. God is faithful. God is reliable, and He knows the beginning to the end. He loves you. He demonstrated that love for you when He sent His only begotten Son, Jesus Christ, to this earth to live for you, die for you, and Jesus rose again from the dead to forgive you of your sins."

"But God demonstrates His own love toward us, in that while we were still sinners, Christ died for us. Much more then, having now been justified by His blood, we shall be saved from wrath through Him."
(Romans 5:8-9)

Let me show how your insistence on an answer makes things worse. I'm writing to you from my own personal experience. Even if God were to explain to you every single detail and nuance of why He's allowed this, and what He's doing exactly, and how it will turn out in the end, you still wouldn't be fully satisfied. It would just create more "what if" and "what about" questions and concerns while you spin your wheels trying to figure out your infinite God. *The better response is to choose to live by faith, trusting God to take good care of your life.* Warren Wiersbe said it best, "we as Christians live by faith, not by explanations."

The so-called trap that the Children of Israel face was not for them at all but for the Egyptians.

"And the LORD said to Moses, *"Why do you cry to Me? Tell the children of Israel to go forward. But lift up your rod, and stretch out your hand over the sea and divide it. And the children of Israel shall go on dry ground through the midst of the sea. And I indeed will harden the hearts of the Egyptians, and they shall follow them. So I will gain honor over Pharaoh and over all his army, his chariots, and his horsemen. Then the Egyptians shall know that I am the LORD, when I have gained honor for Myself over Pharaoh, his chariots, and his horsemen."*

And the Angel of God, who went before the camp of Israel, moved and went behind them; and the pillar of cloud went from before them and stood behind them. So it came between the camp of the Egyptians and the camp of Israel. Thus it was a cloud and darkness to the one, and it gave light by night to the other, so that the one did not come near the other all that night.

Then Moses stretched out his hand over the sea, and the LORD caused the sea to go back by a strong east wind all that night, and made the sea into dry land, and the waters were divided. So the children of Israel went into the midst of the sea on the dry ground, and the waters were a wall to them on their right hand and on their left. And the Egyptians pursued and went after them into the midst of the sea, all Pharaoh's horses, his chariots, and his horsemen."(Exodus 14:15–23)

TRUST

God wants you to learn to trust Him completely, even though you can't see any possible solutions, even though you can't see any way out and you're convinced that it's over. God wants to show you that He alone can make a way where there is no way. God wants to show you He is not limited by man's resources or by your limited capacities. He wants to show you He can do exceedingly abundantly above all that you can think or ask.

"Now to Him who is able to do exceedingly abundantly above all that we ask or think, according to the power that works in us, to Him be glory in the church by Christ Jesus to all generations, forever and ever. Amen."(Ephesians 3:20–21)

This fear in your life has awakened in you a desire to change. *God wants you to learn the value of being His Child, personally.* Everyone in this world faces difficulties, believers and unbelievers alike. The child of God faces them differently, with confidence and hope. Hardships are different for the son and daughter of God. **Nothing is wasted by God.** *He wants you to embrace life's difficulties as part of your testimony, as part of His testimony of grace in you. If God is for you, who can possibly be against you?* When it seems that the enemy keeps chasing and intimidating you, wanting to destroy you and keep you in bondage and slavery, respond with faith. As the enemy is messing with your head, messing with your life, wanting to ruin you simply by trying to chase you down, you can stand in the confidence that God will protect you.

God will let us come to that place which is seemingly a trap allowing us to feel the full weight of the situation. For His own purposes, God will take us on a journey to a place where there seems to be no human way of getting out so that we can learn to trust in Him and not our human resources. He wants me to exhaust my resources and come to the end myself. *It's at the end myself that I finally cry out to God, and BAM, He's right there!*

There is no need to fear. God is going to see me through. He is my all-sufficient God who is able to deliver me from any trap. The enemy thinks he's won. The enemy might spend every waking moment seeking to trap me. Let him waste His time. God is on my side. Amen?!

Moses here with the nation of Israel in their apparent trap doesn't seek to explain the situation to them. He doesn't try to reason with them. He just tells them to get their eyes back on the Lord. Now!

That's what I'm telling you now in this little book, in love. *Get your eyes back on the Lord right now. Stop. Be Quiet. Look to the Lord. Pause and pray. Thank God for His goodness. Ask Him for His help.* Obviously, you know this already, but this book won't deliver you from your fears. But

God can and will do just that! That's what you will get when you ask for help from me or anyone on the team here at Calvary. We will keep pointing you to the Lord and speak unending words of faith to you, encouraging you to trust in Him.

What if you don't have any immediate help around you? If you happen to be in a place of isolation and cannot ask for help right now, speak words of faith to yourself. Open up your Bible and begin to read it in obedience to God. Don't read it to study or argue, but instead, read to walk with Jesus and learn of His love for you. I know you can look back in the history of your life and see God's faithfulness. You can remember times when God used that situation and got you out of that other one and remember how He's brought you to today.

God will continue to remain faithful in your life. He hasn't brought you this far just to drop you. He won't drop you. He will complete the work He's begun in your life.

"for your fellowship in the gospel from the first day until now, being confident of this very thing, that He who has begun a good work in you will complete it until the day of Jesus Christ;."(Philippians 1:5–6)

Part of what God was doing with Israel was to make His name known among the nations. He told Moses He would intervene. He also told him that he would use this time to get the nation in and deal with Pharoah.

It's amazing how God chose to deliver them. He chose a miracle. He chose something that no one anywhere could have possibly considered. He chose to deliver them in a way where no one could take the credit. He chose to split the Red Sea for freedom so that the waters would return to take out the pursuing enemies.

"Now it came to pass, in the morning watch, that the LORD looked down upon the army of the Egyptians through the pillar of fire and cloud, and He troubled the army of the Egyptians. And He took off their chariot wheels so that they drove them with difficulty; and the Egyptians said, "Let us flee from the face of Israel, for the LORD fights for them against the Egyptians."

Then the LORD said to Moses, *"Stretch out your hand over the sea, that the waters may come back upon the Egyptians, on their chariots, and their horsemen."* And Moses stretched out his hand over the sea; when the morning appeared, the sea returned to its full depth while the Egyptians were fleeing into it. So the LORD overthrew the Egyptians in the midst of the sea. The waters then returned and covered the chariots, the horsemen, and all the army of Pharaoh that came into the sea after them. Not one of them remained. *But the children of Israel had walked on dry land in the midst of the sea, and the waters were a wall to them on their right hand and their left. The LORD saved Israel that day out of the hand of the Egyptians, and Israel saw the Egyptians dead on the seashore. Thus Israel saw the great work which the LORD had done in Egypt; so the people feared the LORD, and believed the LORD and His servant Moses."* (Exodus 14:24–31)

God does what he's going to do whether you cooperate with Him or not. The plan of redemption for the nation of Israel existed despite their fears, complaining, and murmuring. You can choose to freak out over the situation or decide to trust in the Lord. He's going to work it all out. The question is will you be in the right position to enjoy it?

DRY GROUND/LAND

In this miracle of passing through the Red Sea and God destroying the enemy, something is almost always missed and glossed over. I want you to take out your Bible and mark in Exodus 14 how many times ***"dry ground or dry land"*** is mentioned. Yes, that is a great miracle in itself. The people didn't slog through the mud, barely making it, losing a few along the way. NO! They marched triumphantly or ran on dry ground. God made a way through for them and made it easier to cross. I love my Jesus, don't you!? He went above and beyond in His delivering power.

"But as it is written: "Eye has not seen, nor ear heard, Nor have entered into the heart of man The things which God has prepared for those who love Him."(1 Corinthians 2:9)

God deliberately led them to this difficult place. They were there on purpose. God did so that His name would be magnified among the nations. He did it so that nation of Israel would walk forward in confidence and faith. God's plan worked! The Red Sea would be on everybody's mind and heart going forward. We are still talking about the power of God at the Red Sea today.

You know that each of us will pass through many trials and face many traps in our own lives where we are stuck and afraid. There is a real fear. There is serious anxiety.

Jesus would tell us that He has it all taken care of. *He already knows what He's going to do in your life.*

"But this He said to test him, for He Himself knew what He would do."(John 6:6)

One thing that has shaken me from time to time in my own personal walk with Jesus is that: I honestly do with all of my heart believe that God loves me, saved me, changed me and that I will live with Him eternally, being reunited with my son Eddie, my parents, and many others who have gone to heaven before me. I believe it with all my heart! I believe God for the salvation of my soul, but there are so many little challenges that I face where I don't believe. I have many lapses of faith in my life. Amazing, isn't it? Even so, *God is good.*

We don't know what the future holds, but we do know Who holds the future. He has been faithful in the past, and He will be faithful to us in the future. He is faithful to you today.

God has revealed to us in His Word that He is a God who can be trusted. There is no need to fear. It's through these difficult times that God does a special work of revealing His love, care, concern, and power to us. We know that our weaknesses are only opportunities for God to show us His strength. I get to learn that my resources do not limit God. My limitations do not hold him back.

"Fear not, for I am with you; Be not dismayed, for I am your God. I will strengthen you, Yes, I will help you, I will uphold you with My righteous right hand."(Isaiah 41:10)

God speaking through the prophet Isaiah is giving a promise to His people. How much more today for us in Christ!

TIME TO FACE

It's time to face your fears, isn't it? It's time to choose to trust God with your life again like you used to. He is ready to meet you in that place of repentance and humility right now. Come back to Him. He's ready to receive you with open arms and comfort your fearful heart.

As you look to the Lord, you won't be overwhelmed by unreasonable responses to real fears. Instead, you're learning to trust in the Lord. There will be fears, real honest, and rational fears. We won't be able to avoid them. What we will avoid by faith is being controlled by them. Instead, we will abide in Christ, controlled by His love and care for our lives.

"Trust in the LORD with all your heart And lean not on your own understanding; In all your ways acknowledge Him, And He shall direct your paths."(Proverbs 3:5-6)

God is going to see you through because you've put your trust in Him. The enemy who has harassed you for so long is the same one who is being led into the trap, and the enemy will not harass us again. AMEN?!

Maybe God is drawn you to this book just so that you could know the power of God to deliver so that you might commit your life to Him and then experience the

power of God. The very circumstances that more or less pushed you here today are the same circumstances that God ordained because he didn't want you to rely upon yourself anymore, but upon his hand and upon his power to set you free. *So, pray and accept Jesus into your life today! Right now.*

For you believers, choose to trust in the Lord today. Let the faithfulness of God in the past be a present reality to you today.

Connect with Ed Taylor

Mail: c/o Calvary Church

18900 E. Hampden Ave.

Aurora, CO 80013

Phone: 303-628-7200

Websites:

edtaylor.org

calvaryco.church

Email: ed@edtaylor.org

Made in the USA
Monee, IL
14 September 2021